Contents

What Makes a Picture Book?

"Children's books … are one of the few quiet places left where a child can go to be alone, and travel to worlds past, present and future." — Dilys Evans, *Show and Tell*

All readers can remember the picture books shared with us in childhood, the first ones we signed out from the library, and the picture book that gave us the "I can read this on my own!" experience. In this vibrant art form, author and artist work together (often they are the same person) to create a rich and rewarding experience for readers of all ages. David Booth and Bob Barton remind us: "The picture book speaks to most children; it speaks to the child in all of us."

Picture books offer a unique bring-and-take experience to the pages. The words, the visuals, the story, the themes, and the format can lead us to new understandings. In schools, picture books shared by teachers, read with our friends, and chosen independently are the foundation of literature and of the literacy experience.

Here, some author/illustrators of picture books talk about their work. Which statements do you agree with most?

"The idea of a picture book, as a literary art form, carries a number of tacit assumptions: picture books are quite large, colorful, easy to read and very simple in their storyline and structure, not very long and (most significantly) produced exclusively for a certain audience, namely children, especially of the younger variety." —Shaun Tan

"An illustration is an enlargement, an interpretation of the text, so that the reader will comprehend the words better. As an artist, you are always serving the words." —Maurice Sendak

"A book should be a springboard to the imagination." —Marie-Louise Gay

Thinking About… Your Picture Book Experience

- What is your first memory with a picture book? How did you experience this book? What feelings are connected with the book? Now that you are older, have you reread this book?
- What makes a picture book experience special for you?

A Personal Picture Book Inventory

To understand ourselves as readers, it's important to think about what we read and how we read. Everyone has different attitudes, feelings, and interests related to reading.

The questionnaire *My Picture Book Inventory* can be used to reflect on the significance of picture books in your life, how much you appreciate picture books, and how familiar you are with this kind of literature. It might be interesting to complete this survey at the beginning of the year, and then again after experiencing a wide range of picture books. Inventories can be shared in small groups to compare responses and attitudes with others.

Thinking About... Reading Picture Books

- How would you describe yourself as a reader of picture books?
- Do you tend to first look at the pictures or read the words of a picture book?
- What are some things that make a picture book "good to read"?

My Picture Book Inventory

1. Here are the names of some author/ illustrators I know:

2. A picture book I particularly like is _____ because _____.
3. A picture book author/illustrator I enjoy is _____ because _____.
4. I remember listening to/reading this picture book when I was very young:
5. I think it is important to talk to others about picture books because…
6. I usually enjoy reading picture books because…
7. After reading a picture book, I think it is a good idea to….
8. The advice I would give a teacher who wants to read picture books out loud is…
9. I think kids should read picture books because…
10. I would choose to buy a picture book to own because…

---

1. WHY PICTURE BOOKS?

A Springboard to the Imagination

Most picture books are written with vocabulary a child can understand, but not necessarily read. So they tend to have two essential functions in the lives of young readers: they are first read to young children by adults, and then children read them themselves once they begin to learn to read. Some picture books are also written with older children in mind, developing themes or topics that are appropriate for children even into early adolescence.

In our classrooms, students can participate in shared reading/listening with a picture book, and make connections or clarify meanings as they explore and exchange ideas with others through discussion or drama. The picture book can support or extend a curricular theme; can serve as a model for writing; can be the well from which personal stories are drawn; can inspire talk, writing, visual expression. Moreover, picture books can serve young people in their own reading development, helping them come to understand the joy of words, the power of story, and the wonder of illustration.

Types of Picture Books

ALPHABET BOOKS
- A theme or concept is organized in ABC order

Ten Alphabet Books for All Ages

Read Anything Good Lately?, Susan Allen & Jane Lindamen
ABC3D, Marion Bataille
Matthew ABC, Peter Catalanotto
Alphabeasts, Wallace Edwards
The Turn-Around, Upside-Down Alphabet Book, Lisa Campbell Ernst
Chicka Chicka Boom Boom, Mill Martin Jr. & John Archambault; Ill. Lois Ehlert
Superhero ABC, Bob McLeod
Gone Wild: An endangered animal alphabet, David McLimans
M is for Moose: A Charles Pachter Alphabet, Charles Pachter
The Hidden Alphabet, Laura Vaccaro Seeger

COUNTING BOOKS

- Help children to learn numbers and number sense

Ten Black Dots, Donald Crews
One Some Many, Marthe Jocelyn; Ill. Tom Slaughter

WORDLESS BOOKS

- Help develop a flexible interpretation of and response to story through pictures

Picturescape, Elisa Gutierrez
Flotsam, David Wiesner

PICTURE STORY BOOKS

- Intricate blending of picture and fiction

Into the Forest, Anthony Browne
The Paperbag Princess, Robert Munsch; Ill. Michael Martchenko

POEMS AS PICTURE BOOKS

- Provide visual interpretation of verbal imagery

Jabberwocky, Lewis Carroll; Ill. Christopher Myers
There Were Monkeys in the Kitchen, Sheree Fitch

TRADITIONAL TALES

- Tales from different cultures, in different versions (including contemporary tellings and parodies)

The Enormous Potato, Aubrey Davis
Lon Po Po, Ed Young

INFORMATION PICTURE BOOKS

- Support a wide range of curriculum areas

Let's Talk About Race, Julius Lester
Ten Things I Can Do to Help My World, Melanie Walsh

GRAPHIC PICTURE BOOKS

- Use comic-strip format, including speech bubbles and narrative

Communication, Aliki
Greek Myths, Marcia Williams

POP-UP BOOKS

- Element of surprise and discovery; sophisticated paper engineering

Yellow Square, David A. Carter
The Wizard of Oz, Robert Sabuda

Thinking about... Classifying Picture Books

- How might you classify the picture books in your library/classroom?
- What category would you add to the list on these pages?
- What titles can you add to each of these categories?

Patterns

Predictable or patterned books have a strong rhythmic pattern in the language that helps the reader predict what will be written and what will happen, providing motivation and satisfaction. Patterned picture books are important for shared reading and initial reading instruction.

Type of Pattern/How to Use/Example	Other Books with Pattern
Repeated Words, Phrases, Stanzas • Repetition helps learning readers join in and read predictable text Slowly, slowly, slowly, a sloth crawled along a branch of a tree. Slowly, slowly, slowly, the sloth ate a leaf. Slowly, slowly, slowly, the sloth fell asleep. — *"Slowly, Slowly, Slowly," said the Sloth*, Eric Carle	*Would you rather…*, John Burningham *Hooray for Fish*, Lucy Cousins *Once Upon a Golden Apple*, Jean Little & Maggie DeVries; Ill. Phoebe Gilman *We're Going On a Bear Hunt*, Michael Rosen; Ill. Helen Oxenbury
Rhythm and Rhyme • Read aloud so students can hear and learn rhyme patterns • Students use the cloze technique to join in and read rhyming words One day a boy woke up with a bunny on his head. He named him Fred, This bunny on his head — *A Boy and His Bunny* by Sean Bryan	*Mrs. Wishy-Washy*, Joy Cowley (series) *Jillian Jiggs*, Phoebe Gilman *Have You Seen Birds?*, Joanne Oppenheim; Ill. Barbara Reid (sequel: *Have You Seen Bugs?*) *Off We Go!*, Jane Yolen; Ill. Laurel Molk

Type of Pattern/How to Use/Example	Other Books with Pattern
Syntactic Structure • Students imitate the pattern of the text in own writing • Readers identify the adjectives, nouns, and verbs Meena lives in India. Meena says *shanta* (shahn-tee). Emily lives in America. Emily says *peace*. — *Can You Say Peace?*, Karen Katz	*A Dark, Dark Tale*, Ruth Brown *Jack's Talent*, Maryann Cocca-Leffler *Round Like A Ball*, Lisa Campbell Ernst *Somewhere Today: A Book of Peace*, Shelley Moore Thomas
Cumulative Sequence • Readers revisit and reread sentences they've already met This is the house that Jack built. This is the cheese that lay in the house that Jack built. — *This Is the House that Jack Built*, Simms Tabak	*Bringing the Rain to Kapiti Plain*, Verna Aardema *The Cake That Mack Ate*, Maryann Kovalski *The Little Old Lady Who Was Not Afraid of Anything*, Linda Williams; Ill. Megan Lloyd *The Napping House*, Audrey Wood; Ill. Don Wood

Type of Pattern/How to Use/Example	Other Books with Pattern
Cause and Effect • Students can predict what they think will happen, and then confirm predictions First the egg / then the chicken First the tadpole / then the frog — *First the Egg*, Laura Vaccaro Seeger	*The Big Sneeze*, Ruth Brown *Something from Nothing*, Phoebe Gilman *If You Give a Moose a Muffin*, Laura Numeroff; Ill. Felicia Bond (series) *Joseph Had an Overcoat*, Simms Tabak
Song • Familiarity of song helps reader decode print I ain't gonna paint no more, no more, I ain't gonna paint no more. But I just can't stand Not to paint my… HAND! Now I ain't gonna paint no more. — *I Ain't Gonna Paint No More*, Karen Beaumond; Ill. David Catrow	*Hush Little Dragon*, Boni Ashburn; Ill. Kelly Murphy *EIEIO*, Gus Clarke *The Wheels on the Bus*, Maryann Kovalski (also: *The Wheels On the Bus*, Paul Zelinsky) *There Was an Old Lady Who Swallowed a Fly*, Simms Tabak
Opposites • Turning the page (usual format) to determine the opposite helps to build prediction • Builds vocabulary as students learn homonyms hot piggies/ cold piggies clean piggies/ dirty piggies — *Piggies*, Audrey Wood	*Olivia's Opposites*, Ian Falconer *Over Under*, Marthe Jocelyn; Ill. Tom Slaughter *Black? White! Day? Night!*, Laura Vaccaro Seeger *Night/Day: A Book of Eye-catching Opposites*, Herve Tullet

Type of Pattern/How to Use/Example	Other Books with Pattern
Question and Answer • Answer questions presented by the author, thus accessing prior knowledge and experience • Understand how sentence patterns work (question and statement) What do you do with ears like this? If you're a jackrabbit you use your ears to keep cool. If you're a bat you 'see' with your ears. — *What Do You Do With a Tail Like This?*, Steve Jenkins and Robin Page	*Brown Bear Brown Bear: What Do You See?*, Bill Martin Jr.; Ill. Eric Carle (sequels: *Baby Bear; Panda Bear; Polar Bear*) *What Does Peace Feel Like?*, V. Radunsky *It Looks Like Spilt Milk*, Charles G. Shaw *I Went Walking*, Sue Williams
Story Shapes • Familiar story shape can help reader grasp sequence of events On Monday, Red Mouse went first to find out. "It's a pillar," he said. No one believed him. — *Seven Blind Mice*, Ed Young	*Mr. Gumpy's Outing*, John Burningham *Good News! Bad News!*, Colin McNaughton *Red is Best*, Kathy Stinson; Ill. Robin Baird Lewis *Alexander and the Horrible, Terrible, No Good, Very Bad Day*, Judith Viorst; Ill. Ray Cruz

2. PICTURE BOOKS FOR LEARNING

Selecting for the Classroom

When selecting picture books, we must consider the literary journey every reader takes in learning to read.

PICTURE BOOKS FOR THE PRIMARY YEARS (AGES 4–8)

- The initial enthusiasm that beginning readers feel about reading must be supported by high-quality easy readers, and balanced by stories and books rich in language and image.
- Be cautious when matching children with books that they want to read and they can also handle.

PICTURE BOOKS FOR THE MIDDLE YEARS (AGES 8–11)

- Today there is a variety of picture books that appeal to older, visually sophisticated students, and to struggling readers and second-language learners who learn more readily using books with more illustrations and less text than traditional texts.
- Choosing books that children themselves may not pick brings a multi-leveled approach to the process of finding out.

PICTURE BOOKS FOR OLDER READERS (AGES 12+)

- Picture books are no longer the domain of the very young. With older readers it is important that the book engage them not only with powerful visuals, but also with a story that has universal, archetypal, or strong emotional appeal.

- In the classroom, picture books are useful to promote core values that underpin the curriculum. They also provide ideal material to enrich students' visual literacy.

Ten Picture Book Pioneers

Eric Carle	James Marshall
Tomie de Paola	Mercer Mayer
Ezra Jack Keats	Dr. Seuss
Leo Lionni	Maurice Sendak
Arnold Lobel	William Steig

Thinking about… Choosing Picture Books

- After reading a picture book, what will readers have learned about reading? About language? About the world? About themselves?
- Many picture books are written by celebrities. Do we buy these books because of the popularity of the author or because of the quality of the story?
- Do you think picture books are only for young children? Why might older readers/adults be interested in reading and/or owning a picture book?

PICTURE BOOK AUTHORS AND ILLUSTRATORS HALL OF FAME

Canadian	British	Australian	American		
Paulette Bourgeois	Allan and Janet Ahlberg	Pamela Allen	Jan Brett	Thomas Locker	Laura Vaccaro
Kady MacDonald	Anthony Browne	Jeannie Baker	Eve Bunting	David McPhail	Seeger
Denton	John Burningham	Graeme Base	David Carter	Barry Moser	Peter Sis
Mary-Louise Gay	Babette Cole	Mem Fox	Peter Catalanotto	Bernard Most	David Shannon
Phoebe Gilman	Lucy Cousins	Robert Ingpen	Doreen Cronin	Jon J. Muth	Lane Smith
Marthe Jocelyn	Michael Foreman	Alison Lester	Leo and Dianne Dillon	Christopher Myers	Simms Tabak
Maryann Kovalski	Emily Gravett	John Marsden	Lois Ehlert	Dav Pilkey	Chris Van
Jean Little	Colin and Jacqui	Shaun Tan	Ian Falconer	Jerry Pinkney	Allsburg
Robert Munsch	Hawkins	Julie Vivas	Mordicai Gerstein	Patricia Polacco	David Wiesner
Stéphane Poulin	Charles Keeping	Jenny Wagner	Kevin Henkes	Chris Raschka	Mo Willems
Barbara Reid	Tony Ross	Margaret Wild	Tana Hoban	Peter H. Reynolds	Jane Yolen
Ian Wallace	Rosemary Wells		Steve Jenkins	Robert Sabuda	Ed Young
Mélanie Watt	Marcia Williams		Steven Kellogg	Jon Scieszka	
Frieda Wishinsky					

Nine Top-Ten Lists

TEN GREAT PICTURE BOOKS FOR AGES 0–5

Jazzy in the Jungle, Lucy Cousins
Goodnight, Me, Andrew Daddo; Ill. Emma Quay
In My World, Lois Ehlert
Where is the Green Sheep?, Mem Fox; Ill. Judy Horacek
Orange Pear Apple Bear, Emily Gravett
A Good Day, Kevin Henkes
Not a Box, Antoinette Portis
Gallop, Robert Butler Seder
First the Egg, Laura Vaccaro Seeger
Knuffle Bunny, Mo Willems

TEN GREAT PICTURE BOOKS FOR GRADES 1–3

Cloudland, John Burningham
Stellaluna, Janell Cannon
The Name Jar, Yangsook Choi
Eddie's Dream, Miriam Cohen; Ill. Adam Cohen
Wilfred Gordon McDonald Partridge, Mem Fox; Ill. Julie Vivas
How to Catch a Star, Oliver Jeffers
Reading Makes You Feel Good, Todd Parr
Smash! Crash!, Jon Scieszka; Ill. David Shannon
Pete's A Pizza, William Steig
Don't Let the Pigeon Drive the Bus, Mo Willems

TEN GREAT PICTURE BOOKS FOR GRADES 4–6

The Dust Bowl, David Booth; Ill. Karen Reczuch
Voices in the Park, Anthony Browne
Fly Away Home, Eve Bunting; Ill. Ronald Himler
My Name is Bilal, Asma Mobin-Uddin; Ill. Barbara Kiwak
The Snow Leopard, Jackie Morris
Yo! Yes?, Chris Raschka
Wabi Sabi, Mark Reibstein; Ill. Ed Young
Grandfather's Journey, Allen Say
Rimshots, Charles R. Smith Jr.
The Red Tree, Shaun Tan

TEN GREAT PICTURE BOOKS FOR GRADES 7+

Life Doesn't Frighten Me At All, Maya Angelou; Ill. Jean-Michel Basquiat
Riding the Tiger, Eve Bunting
Imagine a Day (trilogy), Rob Gonsalves
Rose Blanche, Roberto Innocenti
Prayer for the Twenty-First Century, John Marsden
The Three Questions, Jon J. Muth
The Composition, Antonio Skarmeta; Ill. Alfonso Ruano
The Arrival, Shaun Tan
Varmints, Helen Ward; Ill. Marc Craste
Woolves in the Sitee, Margaret Wild

HA! HA! HA!

Cloudy with a Chance of Meatballs, Judi Barrett; Ill. Ron Barrett
I Ain't Gonna Paint No More!, Karen Beaumont; Ill. David Catrow
Click, Clack, Moo: Cows that Oink (series), Doreen Cronin; Ill. Harry Bliss
The Dumb Bunnies (series), Sue Denim; Ill. Dav Pilkey
Olivia (series), Ian Falconer
Lilly's Purple Plastic Purse, Kevin Henkes
Knock! Knock!, Peter Reynolds et al.
Hooray for Diffendoofer Day!, Dr Seuss & Jack Prelutsky; Ill. Lane Smith
A Bad Case of Stripes, David Shannon
Chester, Mélanie Watt (sequel: *Chester's Back*)

BULLYING

Willy the Champ, Anthony Browne
Hooway for Wodney Wat, Helen Lester; Ill. Lynn Munsinger
Trouble Talk, Trudy Ludwig; Ill. Mikela Prevost (also: *My Secret Bully*)
Say Something, Peggy Moss; Ill. Lea Lyon
Our Friendship Rules, Peggy Moss & Dee Dee Tardiff; Ill. Alissa Imre Geis
Enemy Pie, Derek Munson; Ill. Tara Calahan King
The Recess Queen, Alexis O'Neill; Laura Huliska-Beith
Monster Mama, Liz Rosenberg; Ill. Stephen Gammell
Is It Because?, Tony Ross
Don't Laugh At Me, Steve Seskin & Allen Shamblin; Ill. Glin Dibley

THE GRAPHIC PICTURE BOOK

A Play's the Thing, Aliki
Superheroes: The Adventures of Max and Pinky, Maxwell Eaton
When Randolph Turned Rotten, Charise Mericle Harper
Sticky Burr, John Lechner
Countdown to Kindergarten, Alison McGhee; Ill. Harry Bliss

Pssst!, Adam Rex
Let's Play in the Forest, Claudia Rueda
Little Lit, "It was a Dark and Silly Night", Art Spiegelman & Francoise Mouly (eds.)
Alia's Mission: Saving the Books of Iraq, Mark Alan Stamaty
Tales from Shakespeare, Marcia Williams

NONFICTION PICTURE BOOKS

An Egg is Quiet, Dianna Ashton; Ill. Sylvia Long
Diary of a Worm (series), Doreen Cronin; Ill. Harry Bliss
Red Leaf, Yellow Leaf, Lois Ehlert
The Best Part of Me, Wendy Ewald
Wolves, Emily Gravett
Afghan Dreams: Young Voices of Afghanistan, Tony O'Brien & Mike Sullivan
Martin's Big Words, Doreen Rappaport; Ill. Bryan Collier
The Wall: Growing Up Behind the Iron Curtain, Peter Sis
Transformed: How Everyday Things Work, Bill Slavin
Moses: When Harriet Tubman Led Her People to Freedom, Carole Boston Wetherford; Ill. Kadir Nelson

A CLASSIC BOOKSHELF

Goodnight, Moon, Margaret Wise Brown; Ill. Clement Hurd
Mike Mulligan and His Steam Shovel, Virginia Lee Burton
The Very Hungry Caterpillar, Eric Carle
Harold and the Purple Crayon, Crockett Johnston
Swimmy, Leo Lionni
Brown Bear, Brown Bear, What Do You See?, Bill Martin Jr.; Ill. Eric Carle
The Paper Bag Princess, Robert Munsch; Ill. Michael Martchenko
Where the Wild Things Are, Maurice Sendak
The Giving Tree, Shel Silverstein
The Polar Express, Chris Van Allsburg

3. CHOOSING PICTURE BOOKS

Sharing the Picture Book Experience

> "Reading aloud and talking about what we're reading sharpens children's brains." —Mem Fox, *Reading Magic*

Reading picture books aloud to young people encourages literacy, promotes reading skills, and contributes to the sharing of literature. Hearing text being read aloud allows students —no matter what their stage of reading ability—to focus on how various types of text work and how authors work in the writing process. When a teacher models the joy and satisfaction that comes from reading, he or she can alter a student's attitudes to and appreciation of the developing journey of literacy.

Children need to hear hundreds of picture books read aloud to prepare them to read themselves. A classroom teacher could choose to read aloud a picture book each day of the week, offering students a smorgasbord of literature to enjoy. Many teachers of young children make the read-aloud an important daily ritual, sometimes reading a number of texts out loud throughout the day. When the teacher reads aloud it is a significant time for meeting together, listening together, learning together. The experience builds community. Remember to revisit and reread titles throughout the year. To encourage text-to-text connections, the picture books can be chosen by author, theme, or genre.

Picture Book of the Day/Week/Month

To make comparisons between the books you listen to, as well as to share your opinions about these titles, you can vote on your favorite book weekly, monthly, and at the end of the year.
- A calendar can be used to record the title that is read each day.
- At the end of the week, the class revisits the titles that were shared and votes on the favorite. Place a star beside this title.
- At the end of the month, choose the book of the month. Draw a circle around the winner.

TEN PICTURE BOOKS FOR THE TEACHER TO READ ALOUD
Little Beauty, Anthony Browne
The Black Book of Colors, Menena Cottin & Rosanna Faria
The Gruffalo, Julia Donaldson; Ill. Axel Scheffler
The Flower, John Light; Ill. Lisa Evans
Thank You, Mr. Falker, Patricia Polacco
The Relatives Came, Cynthia Rylant; Ill. Stephen Gammell
Scaredy Squirrel (series), Mélanie Watt
Fox, Margaret Wild; Ill. Ron Brooks
Please, Louise!, Frieda Wishinsky; Ill. Mary-Louise Gay
Owl Moon, Jane Yolen; Ill. John Schoenherr

Ten Tips for Reading Aloud a Picture Book

1. Although the books you choose to read aloud should be appropriate and relevant to the needs and wants of your listeners, choose titles that appeal to you, so you can share your enthusiasm for the book with your audience.
2. Choose a title that listeners might not read on their own. Following the read-aloud experience, students should be motivated to read the book independently, and to read other titles by the author or other books in the genre, or on a similar theme or topic.
3. Draw attention to the format. Encourage examination of the illustrations, although not all pictures have to be shown. Do the illustrations enhance the verbal text? Does the story stand on its own without the pictures?
4. Rehearse the stories you plan to read.
5. Set a context for sharing the picture book. Discuss the title, the cover illustration. Share information about the book or the author.
6. Before reading the book, activate prior knowledge and experience to motivate listeners to make connections. Invite them to make predictions by examining the cover page or the lead page. Take a picture walk through the book.
7. Develop performance strategies that invite listeners into the story. Use dynamic shifts in volume and fluctuations in your tone of voice. Develop character voices that can be used in a number of stories.
8. Find places to pause and ask questions or make observations. Invite spontaneous discussion from the whole group, or have listeners turn-and-talk to respond to a question.
9. Use the think-aloud process. Tell what is going on inside your head as you read the book aloud. This is a useful demonstration of strategies that good readers use to make meaning from text.
10. Most often we can finish reading a picture book aloud at one sitting. On some occasions you might read part of the book and invite oral or written, artistic or drama response. It is also important to reread the book after an initial reading. Don't be satisfied with "we have already read this." Revisiting, reviewing, and refocusing can lead to deeper response.

Thinking About… Picture Books Aloud

- Do you prefer to listen to a book that is read out loud or to read it privately?
- When we listen to a picture book being read, are we "reading"?
- What is your first memory of listening to a picture book being read to you?
- Why is reading aloud a good thing for a parent or teacher to do?

4. PICTURE BOOKS OUT LOUD

Experiencing Picture Books

When you express your personal responses to the picture books you read, you demonstrate your growth as a literature learner. Response activities allow readers to "open up" the text for examining, for questioning, for connecting. Students responding to a picture book can predict, make inferences, respond critically, and develop a sense of story.

We can talk about a book, read parts of the book out loud, raise questions about the book, dramatize scenes from a story, create alternative illustrations for the book, investigate information about the author on the Internet, or become picture book reviewers. We can talk or write about the things that the book reminds us of—the best response to a story is to tell another story. Another way to respond is to go on to read additional picture books by an author, or on a theme or topic.

Responding During Reading

RESPONDING TO VISUALS

Picture book illustrations can surprise us, entertain us, or lead us to new understandings. The visual images have a unique function to support or extend the verbal text.

Our responses to a picture book are often holistic, but careful response to the art that appears in a picture book enhances our visual literacy skills. Use For Art's Sake to become an art critic, as you consider the style and intent of picture book illustrations.

For Art's Sake

1. How does the illustrator's choice of color(s) convey a mood or feeling?
2. What do you know about the medium (art style) used?
3. Do the illustrations give as much (or more) information than the verbal text?
4. Which illustration do you think best matches the verbal text?
5. Which illustration would you like to own? Why?
6. Do you think each illustration is necessary? Explain.
7. If you had to eliminate one illustration, which would you choose? Why?
8. If you could replace the cover image with another one from the book, which would you choose?
9. Is there a picture you would have liked to see included that wasn't?
10. Draw a picture that you think would "continue" the book.

Ten Picture Book Series

Madeline by Ludwig Bemelmans

Clifford by Norman Birdwell

Franklin by Paulette Bourgeois; Ill. Brenda Clark

Arthur by Marc Brown

Willy the Champ by Anthony Browne

Babar by Jean de Brunhoff

Duck by Doris Cronin

George and Martha by James Marshall

Curious George by Margaret & H.A. Rey

Eloise by Kay Thompson; Ill. Hilary Knight

RAISING QUESTIONS

Open-ended questions can serve a variety of functions, including introducing reading tasks by stimulating interest and curiosity, setting up problems that require careful reading, identifying important ideas to look for when reading, and helping readers to construct meaning and initiate dialogue. The questions teachers ask should help students develop higher-order thinking skills that require them to draw on personal knowledge and experience.

Good questions

• Promote discussion, allowing a give and take of ideas
• Provide a purpose for our reading, helping us focus on what the author has said and what the illustrator has created
• Challenge our existing thinking, encouraging reflection

For true learning to occur, students need to be able to pose questions themselves. When readers ask questions, they require a detailed knowledge of the text and need to think deeply about what they have read. Students can increase their questioning powers by drawing on the models we present, but we can also teach questioning as a process that helps them interrogate the text.

The question matrix can help teachers—and students—consider questions that help to look inside and outside the story. Depending on the language that we use, the questions can help readers move to deeper, more critical thinking about the picture books they have heard or read.

Question Matrix

	Who	What	Where	When	Why	How
is						
did						
can						
might						
would						
will						

For more about Questioning see the flipbook *Out of the Question* by Sally Godinho and Jeni Wilson, and *Q Tasks* by Carol Koechlin and Sandi Zwaan.

Responding After Reading

A CLOSE-UP LOOK AT PICTURE BOOKS

It doesn't usually take a lot of time to complete reading a picture book, but it is important to revisit a book to consider the impact the book has had on you as a reader. When looking back at picture books, we can think upon the words, the illustrations, or words and pictures working together to give meaning.

A Close-Up Look at a Picture Book on page 26 presents questions that help you look inside and outside a picture book, inviting you to share your opinion about a picture book you've read. Your views can be shared with others who have read the same picture book, or offered to friends who might choose to read this title.

Thinking about… A Favorite Picture Book Author
- Who is your favorite picture book author?
- What makes this author's work more appealing than picture books by others?
- What questions might you ask an author/ illustrator if he or she visited your classroom?

Personal Response to a Picture Book Read-Aloud

In this activity, adapted from Lynda Hoyt, you use a graphic organizer to write a response after listening to a picture book being read out loud. By sharing your response with two friends, you can find out whether their opinions were similar to or different from yours. This activity works best if you work in groups of three.

1	2
3	4

- Take a blank piece of paper and fold it twice, to make four rectangles. Number the spaces #1, #2, #3, #4.
- In #1, write your response to the book: consider what the book reminded you of; explain your opinion of the book; or raise questions.
- Exchange papers with another person in the group. Read the response that is written in #1. Then, write your response to it in space #2. What did the response in space #1 invite you to think about?
- Repeat the activity one more time. Read both responses on the sheet you receive, and write a response to both in #3.
- The sheet is returned to the person who wrote the first response. Read all three responses on your sheet, and write a new response in #4.
- In your group, discuss the picture book collaboratively. Groups can share their responses in a whole-class discussion.

30 Ways of Working Inside and Outside Picture Books

Using Graphic Organizers

Graphic organizers help us focus on important concepts and see how these concepts are interrelated. Graphic organizers enable readers to identify, recall, and organize details, ideas, and relationships within a picture book using a simple visual format. See the colored boxes over the next few pages for some graphic organizers you might find useful.

OUT LOUD

- Work alone or with others to read the book out loud (e.g., audiobook, readers theatre).
- Retell the story. Retell the story in role.
- Work with others in a Literature Circle to summarize, raise questions, share connections, consider vocabulary, exchange opinions.

Venn Diagram

Useful for making text-to-text connections. Use to compare two books that you have read.

- In the left side of the first circle, list the text features and story elements of one book. In the right side of the second circle, list the story elements of the other book. In the middle overlapping section, list the similarities between the two books.

AUTHOR/ILLUSTRATOR STUDY

- Prepare a list of items that books by an author or illustrator have in common: *How to recognize a book by* _____
- Use a graphic organizer (e.g., Venn Diagram) to compare one or more titles by the author/illustrator.
- Use the Internet to gather and report information about the author/illustrator. Present a profile of your research subject.

WORD POWER

- Investigate new words, favorite words. Create a glossary for the picture book.
- Go on a word hunt for words focusing on a spelling concept (e.g. words of more than three syllables, capitalized words, double consonants) or grammar (e.g., adjectives, verbs).
- Collect sentences or passages that interest you. Create a bulletin board display of these snippets from picture books.

ABC Grid

Work alone or in groups to brainstorm items for each square in the grid. Give yourself permission to leave squares blank, if needed.

- List vocabulary words
- List the titles of picture books
- List the names of picture book story characters
- Prepare an ABC list of ABC books
- List the names of favorite picture book authors and illustrators

a	b	c	d	e	f	g	h

ILLUSTRATING

- Isolate a sentence (or two); create an illustration to accompany this snippet.
- Study the illustrations, considering the medium used by the illustrator and the technique he or she uses to create visual images. Imitating the style of the artist, create an illustration that might have been included in the book.
- Transform the story or part of the story into a graphic text (i.e., comic strip).

WRITTEN RESPONSE

- Summarize the book. What will you tell others about the book in 100 words? 50 words? 25 words?
- Imagine you are a character in the story: what will a diary entry or letter from this character's point of view reveal about this character?

Character Outline

Use this graphic organizer to write words about a character from a picture book you've read.
- Record things that this character did and said on the outside of the outline.
- List words that describe the different feelings that this character might have had throughout the story inside the outline.

- Hitch-hike with the author by preparing a sequel to the book. Or hitch-hike on the pattern, theme, or story to create a new picture book.

DRAMA EXPLORATION

- Prepare a dramatization of the book using improvisation or tableaux.
- Work in role to interview characters who appear in the story. Consider a character who does not appear in the story that you would like to hear from.
- Go forward or backward in time to prepare a scene that would explain a situation in the picture book.

PICTURE STUDY

- Inspect one illustration from the picture book. Prepare a list of all the things you see in the picture.
- Choose one illustration from the book. What does this picture make you think about? What does it make you wonder about, or feel?
- If you needed to eliminate two (or three) illustrations from this picture book, which would you choose? Why?

REVIEW

- Prepare an oral or written review of the book to share with others. Your review can be videotaped, posted on a class website, or run in the class newsletter.
- Create a poster to advertise this book.
- After completing A Close-Up Look at a Picture Book (page 26), work in pairs or small groups to discuss picture books you've read.

GET GRAPHIC WITH ORGANIZERS

- Create a storyboard to show significant events in the story.
- Create a web to tell others about the book: e.g., characters, setting, problem, etc.
- Use For Art's Sake on page 16 and A Close-Up Look at a Picture Book on page 26 to share your response to a book.

Wonder Web

Use a web to brainstorm ideas and questions about a picture book.

- List some questions that you had about this picture book before, during, and after reading the story. Prompts might help you think about things that you wondered about:

  I wonder…
  What if…
  Why did…
  How did…

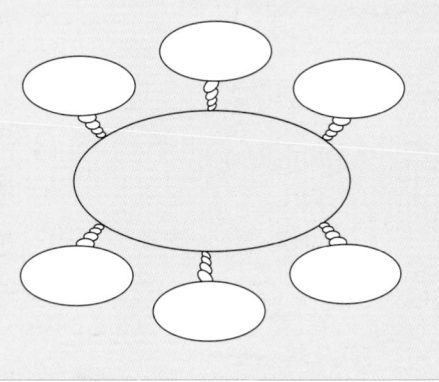

FURTHER READING

- Use the Internet to learn more about the author and the book, to read reviews for the book, etc.
- Collect additional books by the author, or books related by theme or topic. Prepare an annotated bibliography of 6–10 titles: *If you liked this book, then you might want to read _____.* Final bibliography lists can be collected in a binder to be shared with others.
- Read the picture book to someone. Remember to rehearse first!

Storyboard Sequence

Imagine that the picture book you have read is going to be made into a movie. Use words or pictures (or both) to record a sequence of events from this picture book.

- Use three frames to record one scene from the beginning, one from the middle, and one from the end of the story.
- Create a more detailed storyboard, telling the story in six or nine frames.

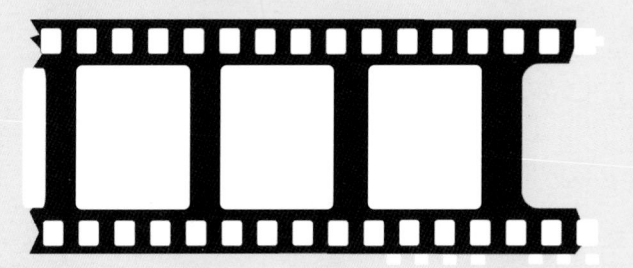

5. RESPONDING TO PICTURE BOOKS

Picture Books for Everyone

No matter what grade level we are involved with, the picture books we experience in the classroom can be read aloud by the teacher, used in guided reading sessions, or read independently. We can choose books from the classroom library, from the school library, or from our bookshelves at home. A student can read a picture book to the teacher, or to someone older or someone younger. Picture books can be read side-by-side with the teacher or a friend, or alone in a private space.

GUIDELINES FOR THE TEACHER

- Provide students with an array of picture books that appeal to a wide range of reading abilities and interests.
- Display picture books in an inviting way, finding ways to advertise and promote a number of titles each day/week.
- Share your opinion about picture books and authors, and opinions expressed by your peers, librarians, and reviewers.
- Allow the students to make their own choices for independent reading. Develop an interest in their choices by having a conversation about books they've read.
- Offer a range of response activities; for some picture books that includes talk, writing, and the arts.

GUIDELINES FOR THE STUDENT

- Browse through several picture books before deciding on one that you will spend time with.
- Develop an interest in a particular author or theme, or books in a series.
- Ask friends, classmates, a teacher, or a librarian to advise you about some picture books you might enjoy.
- Feel comfortable in your reading tastes and choices.
- Keep a log of the picture books you have read (including title, author, topic) and share your opinion of the books.
- Although a picture book may take a short time to complete reading, it's important to revisit the book and to talk about it with others.
- Responding to some picture books in a variety of ways will help develop your tastes and set you on a path for experiencing other kinds of texts.

The Observation Checklist: Growing with Picture Books on page 27 offers you an opportunity to assess the reading behaviors of your students, as well as their involvement and commitment to response activities.

My Picture Book Reading This Term on page 28 will help you consider the kinds of picture books you choose to read and provide an inventory of how important picture books are to you as a reader.

Class Event: A Drama Structure

The introductory pages, or an illustration or short excerpt from a picture book, can serve as a source for drama exploration.

> The wizard watchful, waits alone
> Within his tower of cold grey stone
> And ponders in his wicked way
> What evil deeds he'll do this day.
>
> He's tall and thin, with wrinkled skin,
> a tangled beard hangs from his chin,
> his cheeks are gaunt, his eyes set deep,
> he scarcely eats, he needs no sleep.
> —*The Wizard* by Jack Prelutsky; Ill. Brandon Dorman

Ten Traditional Tales

The Selkie Girl, Susan Cooper; Ill. Mordicai Gerstein
Strega Nona, Tomie de Paola
The Race of the Century, Barry Downward
Glass Slipper, Gold Sandal: A Worldwide Cinderella, Paul Fleischman; Ill. Julie Paschkis
Something from Nothing, Phoebe Gilman
The Name of the Tree, Celia Barker Lottridge; Ill. Ian Wallace
Zen Shorts, Jon J. Muth
The True Story of the Three Little Pigs, Jon Scieszka; Ill. Lane Smith
Seven Blind Mice, Ed Young
Rapunzel, Paul Zelinsky

Strategy	Function	Instructions
Choral Speaking	• to animate print; to explore voice	• group chants the rhyme in a variety of voices; assignment of lines, words, phrases
Discussion	• to share connections; to speculate, predict	• *What do we know? What stories does this remind you of?*
Questioning	• to build commitment; to explore puzzles	• Brainstorming (oral or written) • *What questions might you ask the Wizard (or someone who knows him)?*
Interviewing	• to explore events; to build roles	• Pairs, small groups, or whole class interview in role • *Who might we speak to? Who might be interested?*
Storytelling	• to develop narrative; to build inferences	• Groups tell stories about the Wizard's powers
Meeting	• to negotiate meaning; to problem-solve	• *What should we do? How can we solve the problem?*
Writing	• to explore the present, past, future; to identify with character, dilemma	• Send a letter to the Wizard • Send a résumé to apply for an apprentice position • Prepare a newspaper article about the Wizard's powers

Class Event: The Picture Book Contest

This outline provides a structure for students to use in responding to books through talk and writing as they work alone, in small groups, and with the whole class. Picture books on a range of topics can be used for this activity; however, to help students better make text-to-text connections, focus on a single genre (e.g., humor), issue (e.g., bullying), or curriculum study (e.g., animals).

PHASE ONE

- Reading independently and telling about our choices
- Working alone and then with a partner

Display a range of picture books in the classroom. Invite the students to choose a picture book that interests them. Remind them that, if they don't get their first choice at this time, the books will be available to read in the future. The students read the books independently, then write a response. Two focus questions as prompts: How did you enjoy this story? What might you tell others about this story? Alternatively, students can complete A Close-Up Look at a Picture Book (page 26).

Students work with a partner, telling each other about the book that they have read. Pairs choose which of the two books they think would most appeal to the others in the class. The other book is returned to the display.

PHASE TWO

- Considering criteria for judging a book
- Working with a partner and in small groups (4)

Partners work together, revisiting the book they have chosen.

Two pairs match up, creating groups of four. Each pair talks about their book choice. Each group of four decides which of the two books they think would most appeal to others in the class. The other book is returned to the book display. The groups of four brainstorm a list of criteria to consider for rating the picture book.

PHASE THREE

- Literature Circle discussion
- Working in groups of four

Choose one of the books that has not been chosen as a finalist to read aloud and model a Literature Circle discussion.

Students work in their groups of four for a Literature Circle discussion. Groups exchange books. Volunteers can read the books aloud. The group of four can then discuss why they think this is a good example of a picture book, or not.

PHASE FOUR

- Teacher-led response
- Whole class

By now, there should be four to six chosen picture books. Display these titles in the classroom, and read them aloud over the next week. By the end of the week, the class makes a decision about which book is their favorite. Remind the students of the criteria used to judge a picture book to help frame their criticisms. On the final day, rate the books Gold, Silver, and Bronze winners.

PHASE FIVE

- Responding to a picture book
- Independently, in pairs, in a small group, whole class

The picture book winner can be used as a source for further talk, reading, writing, or art or drama activities. For example: students can create a poster or write a review of the book to share with others in the school or community; investigate other books by the author/illustrator (as read-aloud selections over a week); use the book to prepare a readers theatre presentation; create an additional illustration for the book imitating the style of the illustrator, or write a sequel to the book.

Class Event: Making Books

Many students, young and old, can make picture books of their own and be regarded as young authors. A cooperative picture book can be made in the classroom, with each student contributing a page to the collaborative effort. Young children should be encouraged to complete simple picture books with labeled pictures or simple sentences written on pages that have been stapled together.

To prepare students for this event, demonstrate how words and illustrations are formatted. Patterned and predictable books serve as useful models for students to create their own invented version of a picture book. Moving from draft to publication often requires a number of days to complete.

Ten Steps to Publishing your Writing

1. How will the work be published?
2. Who will be the audience for this book?
3. Have you prepared one or more drafts to ensure that errors in spelling, grammar, or punctuation have been addressed?
4. How many pages will be needed? What size?
5. What font will be used to publish the verbal text?
6. Will the words and pictures appear on the same page? Where will the words appear?
7. How many illustrations will be needed for the published picture book?
8. How will the cover design (front and back) invite readers to pick up the book?
9. How will the book be bound (e.g., staples, rings, professional binding)?
10. Where will you include information about the author, the date and place of publication, and a dedication?

Making Books by Paul Johnson is a useful resource that offers more than 30 practical book-making projects for children. *The Ultimate Guide to Classroom Publishing* by Judy Green is an excellent guide for helping students through all aspects of classroom publishing.

6. PICTURE BOOKS IN THE CLASSROOM

A Close-Up Look at a Picture Book

Name

Title of Picture Book

Author _____ Illustrator

Date of publication _____ Publishing information

1. On a scale of 1 to 10, how would you rate this picture book? Explain.

2. Is the text as strong as the art? Are the illustrations as strong as the text? Is there a balance of information between verbal text and art?

3. What is the medium/style of art used by the illustrator? How appropriate is the art to the information?

4. Which illustration(s) had the most impact on you? Why?

5. What would you tell someone about this picture book?

6. Who do you think might be interested in reading this picture book? Why?

7. As you were reading this picture book, what did you wonder about?

8. How appropriate is the title? Can you suggest an alternative?

9. Is the ending of this book satisfying? Explain.

10. Summarize this book in exactly 25 words.

11. Draw a picture you think could be included in the book.

Observation Checklist: Growing with Picture Books

Name _____

		Not yet	Sometimes	Often	Consistently
Student Reading					
1.	Appears to enjoy reading picture books	☐	☐	☐	☐
2.	Reads picture books independently	☐	☐	☐	☐
3.	Chooses picture books appropriately to read independently at his/her level	☐	☐	☐	☐
4.	Chooses to revisit and reread picture books	☐	☐	☐	☐
5.	Reads a wide range of picture books	☐	☐	☐	☐
6.	Has favorite picture books (i.e., favorite author, favorite theme)	☐	☐	☐	☐
7.	Enjoys listening to picture books read aloud	☐	☐	☐	☐
8.	Picture books seem to be important to student	☐	☐	☐	☐
Student Response to Picture Books					
1.	Reads for meaning, moving easily through the text	☐	☐	☐	☐
2.	Contributes to class discussions	☐	☐	☐	☐
3.	Uses specialized vocabulary to discuss picture books	☐	☐	☐	☐
4.	Analyzes author/illustrator style	☐	☐	☐	☐
5.	Notice's text features; checks that illustrations support print	☐	☐	☐	☐
6.	Retells events in text	☐	☐	☐	☐
7.	Relates picture books to personal experiences	☐	☐	☐	☐
8.	Raises questions	☐	☐	☐	☐
9.	Compares picture books	☐	☐	☐	☐
10.	Identifies and explains preferences	☐	☐	☐	☐
11.	Writes about picture books	☐	☐	☐	☐
12.	Uses picture books as models for his/her own writing	☐	☐	☐	☐

My Picture Book Reading This Term

If you were to list all the picture books you read this term, what would your list look like? Have you read a variety of genres? Did you discover new favorites?

Use this chart to record the picture books you've read throughout the term. Compare your chart with one completed by a friend or classmate.

Title of Book	Author	Illustrator	Date Finished	Rating (scale of 1 to 5)

Professional Reading

Carle, Eric (ed.) *Artist to Artist: 23 major illustrators talk to children about their art.* New York, NY: Philomel Books, 2007.

Bainbridge, Joyce and Sylvia Pantaleo *Learning with Literature in the Canadian Elementary Classroom.* Edmonton, AB: University of Alberta Press, 1999.

Booth, David *It's Critical.* Markham, ON: Pembroke Publishers, 2008.

Donohue, Lisa *Independent Reading Inside the Box.* Markham, ON: Pembroke Publishers, 2008.

Evans, Dilys (ed.) *Show & Tell: Exploring the fine art of children's book illustration.* San Francisco, CA: Chronicle Books, 2008.

Fox, Mem; Ill. Judy Horacek *Reading Magic: How reading aloud to our children will change their lives forever,* 2nd Ed. New York, NY: Harcourt, 2008.

Galda, Lee and Bernice E. Cullinan *Literature and the Child,* 5th Ed. Belmont, CA: Wadsworth, 2002.

Godinho, Sally and Jeni Wilson *Out of the Question.* Markham, ON: Pembroke Publishers, 2007.

Green, Judy *The Ultimate Guide to Classroom Publishing.* Markham, ON: Pembroke Publishers, 1999.

Hart-Hewins, Linda and Jan Wells *Better Books! Better Readers: How to choose, use and level books for children in the primary grades.* Markham, ON: Pembroke Publishers, 1999.

Hoyt, Linda *Reflect, Retell, Retell: Strategies for improving literacy instruction.* Portsmouth, NH: Heinemann, 1999.

Huck, Charlotte, Susan Hepler, Janet Hickman and Barbara Kiefer *Children's Literature in the Elementary School,* 7th Ed. Madison, WI: McGraw Hill-College, 2000.

Johnson, Paul *Making Books.* Markham, ON: Pembroke Publishers, 2000.

Koechlin, Carol and Sandi Zwaan *Q Tasks.* Markham, ON: Pembroke Publishers, 2006.

Setterington, Ken and Deirdre Baker *A Guide to Canadian Children's Books in English.* Toronto, ON: McClelland & Stewart, 2003.

Spitz, Ellen Handler (ed.) *Inside Picture Books.* New Haven, CT: Yale University Press, 1999.

Stagg Peterson, Shelley and Larry Swartz *Good Books Matter.* Markham, ON: Pembroke Publishers, 2008.

Szymusiak, Karen, Franki Sibberson and Lisa Koch *Beyond Leveled Books: Supporting early and transitional readers in grades K–5,* 2nd Ed. Portland, ME: Stenhouse Publishers, 2008.

Index